Free Gift!

Want a free gift?

Email us at
betterlifejournals@gmail.com

Title the email "Journal" and we will send you
something fun!

Visit our website for more:
https://lifelabmagazine.com/better-life-
journals/

We are extremely excited and grateful to have you here for this incredible journaling experience.

Journaling has been proven to have many benefits, including:
- Helps replace your negative thoughts and habits with positive ones
- Helps reduce stress and anxiety
- Helps keep your memory sharp
- Helps improve your mood
- Boosts your immune system (you might not believe this but research has found that journaling has a positive impact on our immune systems!)

Those are just a few. There are lots of other benefits to journaling - in fact, Positive Psychology listed 83 benefits! Let's just say that journaling regularly is really, really good for you.

This journal was designed with your best interest at heart - we want you to get the most out of it, and really benefit from it.

However, you do need to give something to get the most out of this: you need to give it your full honesty. You need to be completely open and honest when journaling. But worry not, this journal is a safe space for your thoughts - this is for your eyes and your eyes only, so pour your heart out and really let go.

We humans are naturally good at finding solutions - we are born with this gift. One of the best ways to find these solutions and insights is through questions, and that is what you will do when you use the prompts in this journal. Asking a good question can not just help you find useful insights and information, it can even cause a massive shift that can completely change your life for the better!

Self-reflection exercises like journaling can add incredible value to your life (and that is an understatement!).

We wholeheartedly hope this journal and the daily process will help you get the most out of yourself, and your life.

We are excited for you!

Instructions

Journaling is a deeply personal experience and as such there are no no hard and fast rules to it.

That said, here are five tips that can help you get the most out of your journaling:

1: Be as consistent as possible. It's not the end of the world if you miss a day or just don't feel like journaling on some days, but the more regularly and consistently you journal, the better. Journaling regularly will keep the positive feedback loop going!

2: Jot down the date at the top of the page. This can help you stay on track, and can also be useful for reflection later on, or even in the future.

3: Missed a day? No problem. Just get back to it the next day. On that note, it can be tempting to do more than one day at a time if you miss a day, but resist that temptation. You will get the most out of this self-reflection exercise by focusing on just one prompt a day. That also keeps things simple for you.

4: Journal whenever you feel like doing it - there is no one "best" time to journal. We personally find it easier to journal either first thing in the morning and/or last thing at night, but you pick the time that works for you best.

5: Be as honest as possible. Some days you will feel a bit off, and that is ok. Being honest is key to getting the most out of journaling.

Most importantly, have fun!

Please can you help us? Leaving a review and rating on Amazon means others can discover and benefit from our wonderful books! Please leave a review :)

Let the
journey begin!

What can I do today to be more positive?

What can I do today to be more positive?

____

____

____

____

____

____

____

____

____

____

____

____

____

____

____

What can I do today to be more positive?

What can I do today to be more positive?

What can I do today to be more positive?

What can I do today to be more positive?

What can I do today to be more positive?

What can I do today to be more positive?

What can I do today to be more positive?

What can I do today to be more positive?

What can I do today to be more positive?

____

____

____

____

____

____

____

____

____

____

____

____

____

____

What can I do today to be more positive?

What can I do today to be more positive?

What can I do today to be more positive?

What can I do today to be more positive?

What can I do today to be more positive?

What can I do today to be more positive?

What can I do today to be more positive?

What can I do today to be more positive?

What can I do today to be more positive?

What can I do today to be more positive?

What can I do today to be more positive?

What can I do today to be more positive?

What can I do today to be more positive?

What can I do today to be more positive?

What can I do today to be more positive?

What can I do today to be more positive?

What can I do today to be more positive?

What can I do today to be more positive?

What can I do today to be more positive?

What can I do today to be more positive?

What can I do today to be more positive?

What can I do today to be more positive?

____

____

____

____

____

____

____

____

____

____

____

____

____

____

What can I do today to be more positive?

What can I do today to be more positive?

What can I do today to be more positive?

What can I do today to be more positive?

What can I do today to be more positive?

What can I do today to be more positive?

What can I do today to be more positive?

What can I do today to be more positive?

What can I do today to be more positive?

What can I do today to be more positive?

What can I do today to be more positive?

What can I do today to be more positive?

What can I do today to be more positive?

What can I do today to be more positive?

What can I do today to be more positive?

What can I do today to be more positive?

What can I do today to be more positive?

What can I do today to be more positive?

What can I do today to be more positive?

What can I do today to be more positive?

What can I do today to be more positive?

What can I do today to be more positive?

What can I do today to be more positive?

What can I do today to be more positive?

What can I do today to be more positive?

What can I do today to be more positive?

What can I do today to be more positive?

What can I do today to be more positive?

What can I do today to be more positive?

What can I do today to be more positive?

What can I do today to be more positive?

What can I do today to be more positive?

What can I do today to be more positive?

What can I do today to be more positive?

What can I do today to be more positive?

What can I do today to be more positive?

What can I do today to be more positive?

____

____

____

____

____

____

____

____

____

____

____

____

____

____

____

What can I do today to be more positive?

What can I do today to be more positive?

What can I do today to be more positive?

____

____

____

____

____

____

____

____

____

____

____

____

____

____

What can I do today to be more positive?

What can I do today to be more positive?

What can I do today to be more positive?

What can I do today to be more positive?

What can I do today to be more positive?

What can I do today to be more positive?

What can I do today to be more positive?

What can I do today to be more positive?

What can I do today to be more positive?

What can I do today to be more positive?

What can I do today to be more positive?

What can I do today to be more positive?

What can I do today to be more positive?

What can I do today to be more positive?

What can I do today to be more positive?

What can I do today to be more positive?

What can I do today to be more positive?

www.ingramcontent.com/pod-product-compliance
Lightning Source LLC
Chambersburg PA
CBHW070913160726

48004CB00003B/1347